PEACE

Peace Under All Circumstances

THE 10 QUESTIONS

Peace Under All Circumstances
The 10 Questions

Matthew Brownstein

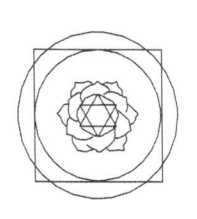

SILENT LIGHT PUBLISHERS
www.silentlightpublishers.com

THE 10 QUESTIONS

Published by Silent Light Publishers.

Peace Under All Circumstances: The 10 Questions
Copyright © 2015 by Anahat Education Group, Inc.

All rights reserved. No part of this book may be reproduced or transmitted in any form or by any means, electronic or mechanical, including photocopying, recording or by any information storage and retrieval system without permission in writing from the Publisher.

Information in this book is provided for informational purposes and is not meant to substitute for the advice provided by your own physician or other medical professional. You should not use the information contained herein for diagnosing or treating a health problem or disease, or prescribing any medication. If you have or suspect that you have a medical problem, promptly contact your health care provider. Information and statements given here are not intended to diagnose, treat, cure or prevent any disease.

Library of Congress Control No. 2005901549

ISBN 978-1518770241

Second Silent Light Publishers Edition

First Edition, 2004

Printed in the United States of America.

PEACE UNDER ALL CIRCUMSTANCES

To You Who Are Peace

THE 10 QUESTIONS

PEACE UNDER ALL CIRCUMSTANCES

CONTENTS

Introduction   1

Questions
1. Who am I?   11
2. Can I handle this?   29
3. Can I be at peace with this?   35
4. What do I feel right now?   43
5. Who is experiencing this right now?   51
6. Have I suffered enough?   57
7. Am I willing to let this go?   63
8. Am I coming from Spirit or ego?   73
9. What is my highest intention in this moment?   83
10. Would I rather be right, or would I rather be happy?   93

Appendices
I. Using The 10 Questions   101
II. Meditating to Know Peace   107
III. Surrendering to Life   121
IV. Opening the Heart and Working Effectively with Emotions   131

About the Author   142

THE 10 QUESTIONS

INTRODUCTION

"It is my intention to have peace under all circumstances."

THE 10 QUESTIONS

PEACE UNDER ALL CIRCUMSTANCES

Over the years of having this experience as a human being, I have found that certain key questions can make an enormous difference between whether or not I live a life of suffering or peace. It is not really the questions themselves that are so important, but rather it is how the questions are answered that makes all the difference in the world.

Our life is happening to us at every moment, and in each moment we walk around with certain assumptions about who we are and how we are to deal with the situations that are put before us. *Peace Under All Circumstances: The 10 Questions* is designed to help us approach life in a way that leads to peace over suffering and love over fear.

We all want to be happy and at peace. No matter what we say we may want, it all comes back to "I just want to feel okay." We may say we want to belong or to be loved or to be admired. We may say we want money or the house or the lover or the new career. However, in the end, all we really want is love. Why is it that we want what we say we want?

THE 10 QUESTIONS

Do we say we want what will make us miserable and upset? Or do we say that we want what will apparently bring us happiness and peace?

We do not really want the things outside of us that we say we want. We only want those things because of the inner feelings that they will bring. We say we want our spouse to love us unconditionally only because we want to feel love all of the time. We say we want a good job with lots of benefits because we want to feel safe and secure. There is nothing wrong with having all the nice things in life. But if these are used as a means of feeling good, we have to ask ourselves, "Is this really the true happiness that we seek?"

Happiness, love and peace are feelings that we feel inside. They do not actually come from the outside.   A person cannot make us feel happy or sad. Rather it is we ourselves who make us feel happy or sad. A situation that might make one person happy would make another very miserable. It is not the external situation, but rather the internal attitude

PEACE UNDER ALL CIRCUMSTANCES

that makes all the difference.

The 10 Questions ask us to question our reality about who we are and how we are dealing with our life. These questions can be taken individually or as a step-by-step process for reestablishing a state of inner peace. Because all we want is peace, The 10 Questions can help to lead us back to this. There is no other goal worth having. The real question is—"Do I want peace in my life under all circumstances or not?"

If your answer is "No," then this book is not for you. If you feel that peace is conditional and that you must make life be an exact certain way to be at peace, then you might not be ready for this book. However, if you answered, "Yes," and said, "Yes, I want to experience peace no matter what," then this book is for you indeed. If you are not sure, then ask Question 6 before continuing on, "Have I suffered enough?"

If you have come to the point where the outside world is

THE 10 QUESTIONS

simply not cutting it anymore and you have realized that all your attempts to create peace are not working, then you are ready to read on. However if you have said, "No, I have not suffered enough and am still going to try to find peace outside by making my life the way I want it to be," then please keep trying. We all want peace in the end. If you have come to the place where you really have made peace your one single goal and are ready to find it under all circumstances, then you are ready for your first question, "Who am I?"

PEACE UNDER ALL CIRCUMSTANCES

QUESTION 1

Who am I?

"I now remember that my true nature is perfect, whole and complete. Who I am is peace, freedom and love. By remembering who I am, I reclaim my Divine Birthright."

THE 10 QUESTIONS

PEACE UNDER ALL CIRCUMSTANCES

What a simple question, yet what an elusive answer. Most of us simply never ask. We live under the assumption that we know. If I ask you who you are, of course you can answer. "Well, I am Joe. I live at this address and have this career. I drive this car and like this and that." Is this who I really am?

Am I my name? Am I my house? Am I my career? Am I my car or my preferences or the sum of my past experiences? If I am sincere, I will have to admit that I am not any of these things. My name can change, but I would still be me. My career or house could change, but I would still be me. I might define myself by the things in my life, but all of that only amounts to a self-concept and nothing more.

A self-concept is not who you are by definition. A concept about a thing is not the thing itself. For instance, if we call the large object that spins around our planet the moon and think that we know the moon simply because of the word "moon," then we are quite mistaken. We may have a lot of concepts about this thing we call "moon" (e.g., big, round, gray, lifeless.) However, is this really the moon as it is? How are we able to know what the nature of a thing truly is? More importantly, how can we know what the true nature of a human being is (i.e., "Who am I really?")

But first we may ask, "To be at peace under all circumstances, why is it important to know who I am?" When we live under the assumption that we are a human being, we are bound to suffer. When we think we are the limited and finite form of the body, then we will suffer tremendously. By identifying ourselves as the body, mind and emotion complex called a *human being*, we are prone to all the ups and downs that occur for human beings. When we assume we are this creature that we have called "human," we become very afraid of change. We know that when things make a human feel good that we want those things, and when

PEACE UNDER ALL CIRCUMSTANCES

things make the human feel bad, we try to push those things away. We live in a state of constant struggle trying to make the world the way we want it to be.

If you were asked, "Are you your body," how would you answer? Would you automatically say yes? What if we removed your arms and legs? Are you still there? Were you made any less? Modern science tells us that every seven years every cell in your body has replaced itself. Therefore, your body is not the same body as it was seven years ago. When you looked in the mirror at five years old and look in it today, are you seeing the same person in any way? Weren't you there looking through those eyes at five observing a five-year-old body? And are you not still looking through those eyes now observing the body at its present age?

We call the body "yours." We say, "My body or your body." This involves a subject-object relationship. If I say I have a thing, I cannot possibly be that thing. If I say I am holding a book, I cannot possibly be the book. If the book

THE 10 QUESTIONS

changed, I would still remain the same. This is important. If you think you are the body, when the body changes (and it will) you will feel disturbed. You like it a certain way; however, inevitably it will change. If your body is you, then you are doomed to suffer and eventually die. However, if your body is not you, then you can simply observe it go through its changes in peace.

It is important to seriously question our relationship with our body. How we answer these key questions determines whether we spend our lives suffering or not. It is important for you to answer these questions for yourself. Are you your body, or are you Spirit experiencing your body?

Millions of people have now reported having near-death experiences where they found themselves floating above their bodies. Countless others have reported out-of-body experiences where they found themselves fully conscious while being apart from their physical form. Even at this very moment, while still apparently in your body, you can observe

PEACE UNDER ALL CIRCUMSTANCES

it. Take a moment and observe your feet. Are you your feet?

If we removed your feet, would you still be there observing? Of course you would. Your body would be different, but you would still be the subject even if the object were gone.

If you are not a thing, you do not have to be disturbed when the thing changes. If you can observe a thing, it does not have the power to change you. You can watch movies or television and, no matter how disturbing the movie, the "you" who is watching is not actually harmed in any way because of the movie.

Now the real secret to peace is to be able to be the observer, not only of your body but also of your emotions and mind. Can you feel your feelings and hear your thoughts?

Most people are totally caught up in their body, emotions and mind. However, even if the whole world argues for their existence as their body, emotions and mind, does this make it true? Are you anger? Are you fear? Are you anxiety? Or are these your feelings?

Do you like red or yellow better? Do you remember your childhood? Are you your preferences, opinions and memories; or are these simply things of which you are aware? Remember the subject-object relationship. If you can observe a thing, then it cannot possibly be you.

It is not my job to tell you who you are. However, I can help you to discover what you are not and help you to come to rest in the truth of your own true nature. I can also tell you what I have discovered about who I am through the process of seriously inquiring into the question.

I can tell you that I am not my body, my body's sensations, my emotions, my thoughts, my opinions, my views, my preferences, my memories, my hopes, my dreams and my intellect. These can be considered mine but are not me. I am the observer of these things. In fact, in truth I have

PEACE UNDER ALL CIRCUMSTANCES

come to know that these things are not really mine at all, but that I am the observer of these things, which are simply energies that float around in the manifest universe.

Because I am not what I observe, I remain unmoved because of these temporary and changing phenomena. However, when a person identifies his or her own consciousness with the object of consciousness, then tremendous suffering is bound to occur. Misidentification with who we really are is the cause of so much pain. Never questioning this, we end up miserable when we try to make the world (including our body, mind and emotions) the way we want.

There is another way—a state of freedom that goes beyond the mere traditional way of being a human being. It simply involves knowing through direct experience who I really am from what I am not. I have come to know very clearly that I am the consciousness that observes form and that I am not the form itself. This is similar to a mirror that reflects many different types of objects. The mirror is not ever changed by what is reflected in it. Whether the object in the mirror is dark or light, pretty or ugly, healthy or sick, the mirror remains unchanged.

Although I cannot tell you who you are, I can tell you what I have come to know about who I really am in my true nature. However, I can attest that you and I are not different in our true essence.

I have come to know that I am the immortal and unchanging soul. I have come to know that my true nature is eternal peace, love and bliss and that this can never change or be taken away. I have experienced directly that who I am is all I have ever wanted to experience and that in my true nature I am eternally one with my Source.

My experience of asking "Who am I?" has helped me to let go of what I am not. It is when we let go of what we are not that we come to rest in who we truly are—and what we truly are is delicious beyond measure. When we think we are human, we say that we are finite, changing, limited, separate

PEACE UNDER ALL CIRCUMSTANCES

and prone to sickness and eventual death. However, when we know we are Spirit, we admit the truth that we are immortal, eternal, unchanging and that we are pure, free and forever.

Admitting this is not a trick of the mind. As we truly begin to explore our true nature, the mind inevitably drops away. In deep meditation, you can transcend your body, mind and emotions and rest in the pure consciousness that you are. What you come to know directly is that you are always there as pure being. You realize that the state of eternal freedom and bliss is not a conditional state that your mind invents, but that it is the inevitable result of realizing who you really are beyond your mind.

Begin by asking, "Who am I?" and deny any answer from your mind that you are a temporary and changing form, whether physical, mental or emotional. Even if your mind tells you that you are Spirit that is not good enough. Remember we want peace under all circumstances. The mind cannot *tell* us that we are peace. We must *know* it for ourselves

THE 10 QUESTIONS

and come to experience it at every moment of our lives.

Once you begin to question who you are, I highly recommend that you take time each day to meditate on your true nature as Spirit. This is so simple and easy. It helps you to become established in the unchanging and immortal Self, rather than the temporary and finite human form. Once you have begun this practice of finding out who you really are, you will delight in the wonder of your own soul. You discover what true peace really is.

If you are suffering, not at peace, not delighting in the experience of life, ask yourself, "Who am I?" At that moment, come back to the you who is observing your body, mind and emotions. Ask yourself if you are this thought, that feeling or that situation that you are observing. The answer is always "No." If you think the answer is "Yes," you are misidentified with something that is changing and temporary, which is subject to pain. When you remember that you are the soul, you are eternally free.

PEACE UNDER ALL CIRCUMSTANCES

The more you practice coming back to yourself, the less you suffer. Whenever you are suffering, ask yourself, "What am I forgetting right now?" The answer is, "I am forgetting that I am the blissful immortal soul who can transcend all pain, suffering and death."

It is only my job to remind you that you are the soul and in truth you already know this. I cannot teach you anything about you that you do not already know deep inside. I can only remind you to come back at every moment to the Divine spark of consciousness that you really are and to live eternally free in that state of pure grace.

THE 10 QUESTIONS

QUESTION 2

Can I handle this?

"I am fully capable of handling any situation that life puts before me."

THE 10 QUESTIONS

PEACE UNDER ALL CIRCUMSTANCES

Having established that you are not what you are observing, we can also establish that this "you" is observing something. Life is a series of moments between birth (meaning the time you came into the body) and death (meaning the time that you will leave the body). In case you haven't noticed, things will happen to you, the soul, while you are having this human experience.

Now you are not the things that happen to you, and you are not the body, mind and emotions that interact with these things. You are the one who is here watching. Experiences will happen to you while you are visiting this fascinating place called Earth. Now these experiences will be pleasant, unpleasant and neutral. This is inevitable. So while you are here having the human experience, the question is, "Can you handle it?"

Remember, it is not the question that is important, but the answer that you give. Are you a human being who cannot handle this? Or are you the eternal soul who is observing

THE 10 QUESTIONS

this situation who can handle anything?

I am here to remind you that you are Spirit and that you have a choice. You can say, "No, this experience is too much and I cannot handle it." You are free to do that. However, notice what happens when you do. You get scared and feel weak and incapable. When you answer "No," your emotions go haywire, and your body suffers because of it. However, when you say "Yes, I can," the whole experience of the moment changes.

Can you handle this? "Yes, I can" should be your only answer. If you say "No," then you will suffer. If you say "Well, I am just a weak human being who is incapable of dealing with this event," then here again you will suffer. You are not a human being, and you are capable of dealing with this event. Life is happening, and you can handle it.

You may agree that you can handle some of it, but not all of it. If you say that you can only handle some of it, you are making your ability to be at peace totally conditional. If

PEACE UNDER ALL CIRCUMSTANCES

you say that some situations could happen that could be too much for you, you are basically saying that you as the soul are not able to experience something without losing your peace. You as the soul can never lose peace, because you *are* peace. You can forget and tell yourself that you cannot handle something and lose peace, but this is not true. You are the soul, you are peace and you can handle anything that passes before your consciousness.

Having peace under all circumstances does not mean that circumstances will always be pleasant. It simply means that you are the observer of these circumstances and that you are the immortal and eternal soul that can go through anything.

You did not come down to have this human experience expecting it to be all rosy and peachy. Life is a constant interchange of dynamic energies that always move from one pole to another. Things go up and go down. People are born and eventually they die. Bodies are healthy, and sometimes

THE 10 QUESTIONS

they get sick. Money comes and money goes. The question is not whether these things happen, because they have been happening forever. The real question is "Can you handle this?" Answer "Yes, I can" and you have taken your next major step toward being at peace under all circumstances.

QUESTION 3

Can I be at peace with this?

"Knowing that I can handle whatever I am experiencing, I am empowered to choose to be fully at peace with the experience as it is—inside and out."

THE 10 QUESTIONS

PEACE UNDER ALL CIRCUMSTANCES

Assuming you are okay with the notion that you are Spirit and not matter and assuming you can handle this experience called Life, now ask yourself, "Can I be at peace with this?" Why not? What could take away what you eternally are? Nothing can change what is eternal. Only if you answer these questions improperly could you not be at peace under all circumstances. You are the soul experiencing Life, and you have decided that you can handle anything that will happen to you. Now can you enjoy it and be at peace with it? Of course you can. You might say, "Well yes, I am the soul, and yes, I can handle this. But I cannot possibly be at peace with it, let alone enjoy it." You might say that you cannot be at peace if your spouse or child dies. You might admit that you are the soul and that you can handle the event, but never could you be at peace with it or enjoy it.

Remember that not only is your body part of this changing world, but so too are your emotions and mind as well. I am

THE 10 QUESTIONS

not saying that when your spouse or child dies that it will make your heart feel good. When a loved one dies, it hurts. Can you handle it? Yes, you can.

Can you be at peace with it? Yes, you can. You can be okay with the fact that what happened hurt. You can be okay with the fact that what happened was an immense challenge. Peace under all circumstances does not happen for your body, mind, or emotions—it happens for you, the soul. You can observe the beauty in birth and death, in creation and transformation and in sickness and health.

You can be at peace with all that is when you admit that all that is—is what is. When you resist what is, you suffer. When you resist what is, you say, "I cannot handle this or be at peace with it." However, you can handle it, and you can be at peace with it.

Only you can rob you of the peace of your own soul by telling yourself that life is too much to handle and that it can keep you from being happy and at peace. Life is a movie.

PEACE UNDER ALL CIRCUMSTANCES

It is a big dream in the mind of Spirit. It is a temporary experience that you are engaged in. Can you handle it? Can you enjoy the show?

Movies can be comedies, dramas, tragedies and horrors. No one goes to see movies of only tranquil lakes and trees in the country. Life is a 3-D movie, and you have a front row seat. Can you handle it? Can you enjoy it?

It will end, and you can handle that too. Will you enjoy your own death? Will you enjoy every minute of this exquisite experience, or will you resist it and be miserable right up until the very end? If you know you are the immortal soul having a brief trip into time and space and that you can handle the whole experience, you can simply choose to be at peace with it. You are peace, and every time you come back to your Self, you can easily become reestablished in the observer of this incredible drama called Life.

To gain peace under all circumstances, you have to know

where peace is found. It is not found in stopping people from being born, living as they live and then dying. It is not found in manipulating and controlling people, places and things so that you do not have to have your buttons pushed. Any buttons you have will be pushed, now the question again is "Can you handle this?"

Life is full of every possible extreme that you can imagine. It is unlimited in its scope and capacity for expression. It is simply doing what it is doing, and it has been doing it for a very long time, and it will keep doing it for a very long time. Peace is not about changing life to match what you need so as not to feel your emotions. Peace is about changing your relationship to your emotions so that you can feel them when they come up. You will have emotions when life happens, but you will be able to observe your emotions without disturbance.

You can only say, "Yes, I can be at peace with my grief" when you know that you are not the one who is grieving.

PEACE UNDER ALL CIRCUMSTANCES

You are the observer of grief, and in the act of observing you are free from the suffering that comes from resisting grief. Remember that suffering is resistance to what is. Pain will inevitably happen, but suffering is your choice. Peace is the opposite of suffering. You can be at peace by allowing what is to be—including your body, mind and emotions. When you sit back and allow life to be what it is, things not only feel better, but transform in remarkable ways.

So much suffering with negative emotion is simply our resistance to these emotions. When you allow the emotions to be there, you find something exceptional about fully feeling them. Someone dies, it makes you sad. How beautiful is that? Now you are fully having the human experience. It actually becomes nourishing rather than depleting to fully let these emotions be there. Just remember that you are not your emotions and that you, in your essence, are peace. Nothing can rob you of peace, not even your own mind and emotions.

THE 10 QUESTIONS

The key here is transcendence. This does not mean that you leave your body or have to wait until the body dies to know peace in the afterlife. It means that you are the soul who is observing time and space. Are you in time and space or are you observing time and space? The truth is that you are the observer, and time and space are in you, you are not in them. Your body, mind and emotions are in you, you are not in them. You transcend them and therefore you can watch them.

To transcend is not to be detached, cold or distant. It just means that you are not attached. There is a big difference between being detached and closed and being non-attached and open. You can be non-attached and open and still be at peace. The questions to follow will continue to help move you into this way of being.

PEACE UNDER ALL CIRCUMSTANCES

QUESTION 4

Who do I feel right now?

"I choose to keep my heart open and to remain in touch with my feelings as I now choose to experience life to its fullest."

THE 10 QUESTIONS

PEACE UNDER ALL CIRCUMSTANCES

We have established that life is happening and that you are the observer of it. We have also established that you can choose to handle it and to be at peace with it, so now we can ask, "Can you fully participate in it? Can you experience it in its fullness?" Asking "What am I feeling right now?" brings you back again and again to the moment as it is. Your heart must be open to fully experience life. If you close down and ask "How do I want to feel?" or "How should I feel?" then you rob yourself of the glory of the moment. How I want to feel is totally irrelevant. Life is happening, and the human being is having feelings about it. Put your hand on a hot surface, it burns. Lose a loved one, it hurts. If you are told you have a terminal illness, I am sure you will feel something about it.

It is therefore not really worth asking "How do I want to feel?" Rather you can simply ask, "How do I feel?" This question keeps your heart open. It keeps you in touch with your body, mind and emotions. Remember that you are not these things. When you ask "How do I feel?" you are really

THE 10 QUESTIONS

saying, "I am the soul observing the human: What's going on in there?"

It does not have to matter to you what goes on in there. If it does, you will lose your peace. If you insist on only having positive thoughts and emotions, you will become very miserable and very busy. If you only insist on good sensations and loving feelings, you are as good as dead. You cannot have one without the other. Fortunately, you are the soul, and what you are is everything you truly want to feel. Your body, mind and emotions will be what they are—and fortunately so shall you.

When you ask, "How do I feel?" you are remaining open to the experience of life, and what is changing is allowed to change. When you resist your feelings about life, these emotions get trapped and blocked, and you continually make your body, mind and emotions that much more disturbed. If you suppress and deny the human feelings, then eventually the system will become sick and depressed.

PEACE UNDER ALL CIRCUMSTANCES

As you ask "How do I feel now?" open to it. Remain rooted in who you are as the soul and feel your feelings. Feelings have an amazing way of resolving themselves when you get out of the way.

Imagine a pond of water that is muddy and full of waves and ripples. You cannot see your reflection or the bottom, and the more you try to stop the waves and clear the dirt, the worse it gets. If you think about how you want the pond to be or how it should be, and you are silly enough to try to make it that way, you will be very busy and very miserable, because the pond will never get the way you want it through your efforts.

Now imagine sitting on the shore at peace with who you are, knowing that you can handle the fact that the pond is dirty, and knowing that you can enjoy seeing it as it is. Now you ask, "What's going on in there?" Well, it's dirty and unclear. Can you handle it? Of course you can. Just let it be as it is, and it will settle down on its own, and then in time it will get stirred up again.

THE 10 QUESTIONS

Peace does not involve always keeping the pond clear. It involves sitting on the water's edge enjoying what is happening in the ever-changing waters. Peace does not involve making your life, your body, your mind or your emotions "perfect." Peace simply means you can watch the whole experience from the seat of your soul, while experiencing it fully.

When you ask "How do I feel now?" you get to thoroughly embrace your life. You will know all your laughter and all your tears. How beautiful is that? You would not want to avoid this even if you could. To avoid it would mean being half-alive—with one foot on earth and one foot still in the womb.

So many of us do not want to be alive fully. We want to crawl back into our mother's belly and stay in that safe warm place. It would really be much more productive to find the peace of your soul, knowing that you can handle and enjoy life and feel it fully for all its worth. Life is a temporary

PEACE UNDER ALL CIRCUMSTANCES

experience, and no one who came here ever stayed. You will leave this changing world, so while you are here, can you feel it fully? "Yes, I can!"

THE 10 QUESTIONS

PEACE UNDER ALL CIRCUMSTANCES

QUESTION 5

Who is experiencing this right now?

"I am not what I am experiencing right now, and I can rest in the peace of my own being as life continues to unfold."

THE 10 QUESTIONS

PEACE UNDER ALL CIRCUMSTANCES

Assuming that you have inquired into the first and most important question "Who am I?" then you can find profound peace coming when you then ask, "Who is experiencing this right now?"

Under Question 1 we explored the notion that you are not what you are experiencing and that you can be the observer of everything that happens to you without being caught up in it—including your body, mind and emotions. If you ask "Who is experiencing this right now?" you direct your attention back to this "you."

Remember the concept of a subject-object relationship with an "I" and an "it." The "I" is not the "it," and the "I" can remain at peace regardless of what is happening to the "it." For example, say that you were diagnosed with a serious medical condition. First, you could ask yourself, "Who am I?" Are you the illness, the diagnosis or the body that has been diagnosed? The illness, its label and the body in which it resides is not you. If you ask "Who is it that is experiencing this

THE 10 QUESTIONS

illness right now?" you can bring yourself back to that transcendent awareness that can have the experience of the moment without losing your center of peace.

When something challenging happens, like a serious medical condition, you would remember to ask, "Can I handle this?" and you would only answer, "Yes, I can." Then ask, "Can I be at peace with it?" Perhaps this is the hard part. You know you have to handle it, but can you really be at peace with it and even enjoy it? If this is a struggle, then remember Question 5, "Who is experiencing this right now?"

When you come back to your own seat of consciousness, you can observe without being caught up. You can step back and experience what is happening as the subject who is not identified with the object. You can come to rest in the essence of your being which is pure peace, pure love and pure bliss.

You might say that the situation is too difficult to be at peace. Question 5 essentially says, "I remember who I am

PEACE UNDER ALL CIRCUMSTANCES

and that I am peace. Peace cannot be taken from me, because peace is what I am." This changes everything. It does not change your life or your body, mind or emotions, which are still objects of consciousness. However, it does change where your consciousness is located.

Consciousness located in the body, mind and emotions often believes itself to be these things. However, when it wakes up to who it really is, then it resides in its own essence of peace. Remember, whenever something appears to cause suffering, ask yourself, "Who is experiencing this suffering right now?" The question will bring you back to your own being, which resides in the present moment, and help to establish you in the one who is watching rather than in what it is watching.

THE 10 QUESTIONS

PEACE UNDER ALL CIRCUMSTANCES

QUESTION 6

Have I suffered enough?

"I choose only to be at peace as I have suffered enough."

THE 10 QUESTIONS

PEACE UNDER ALL CIRCUMSTANCES

A significant reason why you continue to suffer is that you are often unwilling to let something go that you still feel you need. Perhaps a loved one has died, and you are not willing to accept the loss. A business has failed, and you beat yourself up for not having tried harder. Perhaps you are going through a divorce and cannot bear the thought of being alone. In this case, you may want to ask, "Have I suffered enough?"

It is crucial to come back always to the one who is observing in the present moment. The moment is what is happening now. Your mind insists on trying to make the moment different from what it is, and in this you cause yourself so much needless suffering. When you ask, "Have I suffered enough?" you are essentially saying "I have been through a lot, and there is no need for me to keep perpetuating these uncomfortable feelings."

Remember that the question is not important, but rather how you answer the question. What if you said, "No, I have not suffered enough?" What if you still felt there was some value in holding on to something that no longer served you or that was simply not there anymore? The answer is obvious—you would still continue to suffer.

When you answer "Yes I have suffered enough," you allow change to occur in the direction of freedom from suffering. In that moment you allow compassion and love for yourself to enter into the equation. Perhaps you suffer from a psychosomatic illness in which your mind is a major cause of the problem or where your mind seriously exacerbates the problem. Ask yourself, "Have I suffered enough?" If you have, you are preparing yourself to allow some change to occur.

Remember that the guilty punish themselves. They think they are bad or did something bad and that they need to make up for their past transgressions. They repeat over and over again consciously and subconsciously that they deserve to suffer and that this suffering will somehow bring them

PEACE UNDER ALL CIRCUMSTANCES

peace. At first, this seems so deeply irrational, but we all do it to one degree or another.

When a person feels they have done something that went against their moral principles, they feel they need to atone for this. Often we cannot make amends for what happened, and so we beat ourselves up for what happened in an attempt to rectify the past. This mechanism of guilt causes so much needless suffering and robs us of our peace. The belief that making ourselves suffer will correct a past that no longer exists simply does not work.

Have you suffered enough? Why does your mind believe that suffering will alleviate suffering? Suffering only creates more suffering. Peace only creates more peace. When you have lived with a situational or physical problem for a very long period of time, ask yourself, "Have I suffered enough with this?" If the answer is "Yes" and you can change the situation, perhaps it is time to change it? And if the answer is "Yes" but you cannot change the external situation, then

THE 10 QUESTIONS

ask: "Can I handle this? Can I be at peace with it? Who is experiencing this right now? And haven't I suffered enough by resisting what is?"

Some things will not change in your lifetime. For as long as you live, it will always rain. Day will become night, health will become illness, and birth will lead to death. No one has really changed this so far. Hurricanes, earthquakes and droughts still happen. This is not the problem. The problem is that our minds still feel that by resisting these things we will somehow find peace. We can always work to make the world a more comfortable place to live in, but regardless of our external circumstances the real question still remains, "When will I allow myself to be at peace no matter what is happening?" and "When will I have suffered enough to simply let go and enjoy my life as it is?"

PEACE UNDER ALL CIRCUMSTANCES

QUESTION 7

Am I willing to let this go?

"Through letting go and releasing, I allow what is to be what is as I reside in perfect peace and freedom."

THE 10 QUESTIONS

PEACE UNDER ALL CIRCUMSTANCES

A question that is intimately connected to "Have I suffered enough?" is "Am I willing to let this go?"

Suppose you are ready to stop resisting life and punishing yourself for your past. Then ask yourself, "Am I willing to let go of these ways of being that no longer serve me?" "Am I willing to let go of what is no longer in my life and to let go of the part of me that still tries to repeat the past in the present?"

We need to let go of two major things if we truly want to know peace. One is the outside, and the other is the inside. The outside is the world around us including people, places, things and events—our body, house, career, family, clothing and all the rest of material existence. The inside is our bodily sensations, our mind and our emotions. Both inside and outside are ever-changing phenomena. Inside and outside are not eternal and will never be the same for long. The question is, "Can you let these change, or do you need to try to make the

THE 10 QUESTIONS

temporary eternal?"

In the end we have to let go. The belief that holding on to something will bring us peace is simply erroneous. There is no peace in trying to repeat the past in the present. Peace comes from knowing who we are as the observer of the changing world. Peace does not come from getting caught up in the changing world and trying to make it how we want it to be.

So many of us strive for peace and freedom by trying to make the outside and inside comfortable places. We believe that freedom is getting to be able to make things as we want them. We believe that peace will come once we have accomplished this. It simply does not work. No one has ever found true freedom and peace from manipulating and controlling mind and matter. Most of us are still trying to do this, but we all know deep down inside that it does not work.

Let's assume someone is still trying to find peace and

PEACE UNDER ALL CIRCUMSTANCES

freedom through trying to make inside and outside the way they want. If you ask this person, "Have you suffered enough?" they will answer "No." They still have the insane belief that they will eventually get it right and then they will be okay. Suppose they feel okay because they did get things "right." If you ask if they have suffered enough, they will still answer "No." However, this peace and freedom is conditional and dependent on keeping things a certain way. It is not the peace under all circumstances that we are alluding to here. Peace under all circumstances means that the outside and the inside can be just as they are and that you are okay with this.

True freedom is the freedom from desire. It is not doing what you want and getting what you want, because in the end things will happen that you do not want. True freedom is the ability to love the moment just as it is and to be totally fulfilled from within knowing that you need nothing from without. However, this state is impossible to achieve if we are

THE 10 QUESTIONS

not willing to let go. As long as we are busy trying to create peace, then we will never realize that we are peace.

Again this does not mean that we need to cease living and settle for things. We do not have to live uncomfortably simply to see if we can be at peace there too. The secret is to just keep living and to do what must be done. There are appropriate actions at every moment. Do the dishes not to seek peace from a clean house, but because it is appropriate to keep the house clean.

Suppose that you do not like doing the dishes. What should you let go of—the dishes or the part of you who does not like doing the dishes? Letting go of the dishes and throwing them away would most likely be inappropriate. However, if you let go of the part of you who does not like doing the dishes, you can be at peace, whether you have to do the dishes or not.

Therefore, when you ask "Am I willing to let this go?" you are not necessarily letting go of the outside event, but more

PEACE UNDER ALL CIRCUMSTANCES

likely you are letting go of the internal preference. Freedom is not to make the world match your likes and dislikes, your wants and not-wants, your hopes and dreams and your preferences for and against. Freedom is to let go of these things from the inside.

You would prefer for your children not to die before you; however, this is not up to you. Freedom and peace in this case is not to make your children live indoors all the time to protect them. Freedom and peace is to do what is appropriate in raising your children and to let go of the part of you that is worrying all the time. Ask "Am I willing to let this go?" If you answer "No," you may say, "I am willing to let other people's children be as they are, but not mine. I will not accept certain things happening, and I will be miserable if they do."

I am not condoning irresponsibility in raising children. Of course, you care for your children—this is the appropriate thing to do. I am only asking you to question whether being afraid and worried is bringing you peace and freedom. Freedom is to be okay no matter what happens. Peace is to be okay no matter what happens. Remember being "unconditionally okay" does not mean that your internal state of mind and emotions will always feel good. If you lose a child, it will hurt. Can you handle this? Can you be okay with the feelings you will feel? Can you remember that you are the observer of these feelings? Can you admit that your personal suffering will never change the past? Finally, are you willing to let this go?

I know it can be hard to let go of what we loved and made us happy. However, remember that peace, happiness and love are internal states and that we should cultivate those feelings within ourselves regardless of the external world. When we are full of peace, love and happiness for no reason at all, then changes in our lives are not the cause of suffering in the way they used to be.

We are so afraid to lose what we love, because we think it

PEACE UNDER ALL CIRCUMSTANCES

is the source of our love. We cling to what made us happy, because we did not have happiness within. We strive for external freedom to do whatever we want because we do not feel free inside, and we try to make our environments virtually sterile in an attempt to find peace outside of ourselves. It is only when we know who we truly are that we truly discover freedom and peace. It is only when we are deeply connected to our Source that we can be okay no matter what happens.

A major step in being at peace under all circumstances is that we have to let go. No matter what, no matter how intense life can be, the truth is that you have suffered enough. There is no reason for suffering, and it is indeed a choice. Suffering is resistance to what is. When we let go and let what is be what is, then we cease to suffer and can become reestablished in the "I" who is having this experience called Life.

THE 10 QUESTIONS

PEACE UNDER ALL CIRCUMSTANCES

QUESTION 8

Am I coming from Spirit or ego?

"I now choose to let go and to remain rooted in my true nature as eternal Spirit."

THE 10 QUESTIONS

PEACE UNDER ALL CIRCUMSTANCES

One of the simplest ways to be at peace is to let go of what is not peace and choose to reside where true peace can always be found. There are essentially two places that you, the consciousness, can dwell—in Spirit or in ego.

The ego mind is the you who largely identifies itself with the body, mind and emotions. It is the one who says, "I am a body, I am a mind, and I am emotions." It seldom says, "I have a body, mind and emotions," because it is too busy claiming to be these things. It is the part of your mind that says you are human and not Spirit. It is not bad or evil, it is simply mistaken.

The ego masquerades as if it were you. It says, "I am happy, I am sad, I am hungry, I am tired, I am lonely, I am sick," and so on. The fact that it acknowledges happiness, sadness, hunger, fatigue and sickness is not a problem. The real problem is that the consciousness that you are identifies with it and believes that whatever it says is the

THE 10 QUESTIONS

truth of who you are. You are not your ego. Again it is a subject-object relationship.

Your ego resides in your mind, and you are not your mind. You can observe your mind think, "I like this and I do not like that," but no matter how many times it says it is you—the true self—it is not. It masquerades as you, but it can never *be* you. It will try to establish the feelings that you long for, such as peace, bliss and love; but it never truly can. It only knows about the changing world of form and only can try to find peace there. It does not know true peace and never will.

This part of your mind will always feel separate from all that is. It will always cling to false beliefs and fuel negative emotions. It is a false belief in and of itself because it thinks that it is the real you. Unfortunately you might think it is you as well. It is the "I-sense" of your mind that claims it knows who it is. When the soul rests within it, then the soul thinks it is whatever the ego says. If the ego is happy you are

PEACE UNDER ALL CIRCUMSTANCES

happy; if the ego is sad you are sad. If the ego likes someone then you like that someone; and if the ego does not, then you do not. If the ego is okay with a situation, you are okay; and if it is not, you are not.

When our true self gets caught up in the ego, we suffer tremendously. If the ego believes it can handle something, then we think we can. If the ego is willing to let go, then we can let go. However, when we reside in Spirit and not ego, we can handle anything and let go of anything. Remember when you ask, "Who am I?" and you discover your true self as pure peace and freedom, then you are always empowered to answer all of the other questions correctly.

When you reside in Spirit and not ego, you can observe everything that happens to you, including your own ego, without getting caught up. The true you is eternally free and is perfect peace. The true you is pure consciousness. It can be established in itself, or it can identify very easily with what it is not. We can come back to the idea of the mirror and what it reflects. The mirror can know itself to be the clear, pure and unchanging mirror; or it can forget and think that it is what it reflects. The mirror experiences the forms, but it is not the forms.

The ego is analogous to a person looking in the mirror and saying things about himself. There is a person in the mirror now with a body, mind and emotions. The mirror somehow concludes "I am this person, and if this person is happy then I am happy, and if this person is not happy then I am not." The mirror is always the mirror, even if it forgets.

Remembering who we are is the first step. We come to this by asking "Who am I?" and "Who is experiencing this right now?" Then once we know that we are the observing consciousness, then we must always ask ourselves at every moment, "Am I coming from Spirit or from ego?" "Am I coming from a sense of misidentification with the person in the mirror, or am I just being the mirror itself?" If you are the mirror itself, then you can handle anything and be at

PEACE UNDER ALL CIRCUMSTANCES

peace with everything.

Now imagine answering the questions we know of so far from the perspective of the ego or from the true vision of the Divine Self.

From the ego: "I am the body, mind and emotions and if this human unit which I am is okay, then I am okay. I can only handle things that make me as a human being feel okay, and I am only at peace when the human system is okay. I am whatever I feel right now, and I have not suffered enough because eventually I will get things the way I want them to be. I cannot let go of what made me feel good, because my happiness is conditional on those things."

This is pure suffering and conditional peace.

Now from Spirit: "I am the eternal witness who is pure, free and forever. I am not the body, mind and emotions but observe these from a place of perfect peace. No matter how the human being feels, I am okay. I am at peace in sickness and in health, in happy or sad times, and in all situations I remain forever the same. I am always ready to release the suffering that comes from my identification with the human self and to reside in peace and freedom in my true nature. I easily let go of everything that comes and goes, because I am the immortal and eternal Spirit that remains forever unchanged by the dramas of this changing world."

The choice is always yours. You can choose to reside in the lower or the higher self at any moment. You can choose to be caught up in your humanness and all its suffering, or you can reside in your Divinity in all its glory. However, you can only make this choice when you know you have a choice. If you think that you are just the human being and that there is no other reality to who you are, then you have no choice. You have nowhere to sit except in a changing world that will always contain elements of birth and death, happiness and sadness, and health and sickness.

The choice is so easy once you are empowered with the knowledge of your true self. At every moment you can ask

PEACE UNDER ALL CIRCUMSTANCES

yourself, "Am I coming from Spirit or coming from ego?" If you are suffering, you are coming from ego. If you are looking for love outside yourself, you are coming from ego. If you are trying to manipulate and control others, you are coming from ego. You never have to do this. If you choose to live in Spirit and to keep your consciousness there all of the time, then your life will only improve and your internal state of peace will become unwavering and permanent. The choice is always yours.

THE 10 QUESTIONS

PEACE UNDER ALL CIRCUMSTANCES

QUESTION 9

What is my highest intention in this moment?

"My only intention is to reside in the peace and freedom of my true nature."

THE 10 QUESTIONS

PEACE UNDER ALL CIRCUMSTANCES

This is such an important question. It helps us to become rooted in a place of pure peace again and to unravel the faulty logic of our ego mind. When we ask, "What is my highest intention in this moment?" we have to question seriously if our intention is to be at peace or not. You may think that you have many intentions, but ask yourself at every moment "What is my highest intention?" The ego will say it wants to have a baby, get a new job or buy a new home. It will tell you that you are good, or it might say that you are bad. It can tell you that you are sick or that you are healthy. The truth is that it really does not matter what it says, because it is not you. Being at peace under all circumstances does not mean that the ego is always positive and loving; because, if the ego is not positive and loving, we cannot be at peace. The highest intention is to be at peace, even when the ego is telling us that we are not.

The ego is a thought being reflected in the mirror that

THE 10 QUESTIONS

thinks it is a separate self. It is not a separate self and it is not you. It really does not matter what that part of your mind says if you are able to watch it and not be caught up in it. When you are caught up in it, you will try to make it think positive and be optimistic. You will try to make it loving, kind and even spiritual. No matter how "spiritual" the thoughts of the ego are, they can never be the Spirit that you are. The secret is not to fix the ego. The real secret is to transcend it and to let it go.

An amazing way to let go of this part of your mind is to question its intentions. When it says something like, "What you did was wrong, and you now do not deserve to feel good," then you can ask that part of your mind, "What do you want most for me? What is your highest intention?" This part might answer back, "Well, what you did was wrong, and you should be punished for it." Then ask it, "Why would you want that? What is your highest intention for me?" It will then say something like, "You should be punished to atone for your

PEACE UNDER ALL CIRCUMSTANCES

sins."

Still that is not its highest intention, so you ask it again, "Why would you want that?" "Because if you atone for your sins, you will become a good person again. I am trying to make you good by punishing you." Then ask it again, "Why would you want me to be a good person?" To which it will finally reply something like, "Because I want you to get into heaven in the afterlife," or "Because I want you to do good now so you can live a happy life."

In the end, the ego only wants peace. However, it is mistaken in thinking that it will get peace through suffering. It believes that by making the finite infinite that it will always have what it wants. It believes that by making the changing unchanging that it will create some sense of security and peace. It only wants what you already are and is desperately trying to find this peace and freedom, but it is doing this in ways that do not work.

When you ask, "What is my highest intention in this

moment?" the only one true and correct answer is, "I want peace." You might use other synonyms like, "Love, God, Truth, Oneness or Bliss," but in essence you are saying the same thing. You only want people, places and things to be a certain way so you can have peace. The irony is that you already *are* peace. Remember peace is not something to establish—peace is something that you come back to. It is already there, only you have been "lookin' for love in all the wrong places!"

Ask "What do I want right now?" and then ask yourself, "And why do I want that?" When you can answer that question, then your happiness is conditional. When you cannot answer that question, then your happiness is complete. This means that when you say, "I want a new spouse," that you can answer the question, "And why do I want a new spouse." It does not matter what you answer. Just the fact that there is an answer to that question means that your happiness from wanting this thing will be conditional.

PEACE UNDER ALL CIRCUMSTANCES

You might say "I want a spouse because I have children who need a father, and I want someone to love and provide for me." And why do you want that? The answers will keep coming until you come to the place where you admit that you simply want to feel love and peace. Again, this does not mean that you do not get married or provide a father for your children. It only means that you know what you really want so that you can have it.

When you honestly say, "I simply want to feel love, peace, happy or truly okay," then you cannot really say why. There is no real answer for this. Why do you want to feel love? You want to feel it because you are love. When you are not in touch with who you are, you suffer from the belief that you lack something essential. You do not lack love, peace and joy. You simply have been looking for these in the wrong places. These feelings can be found right within your own being—your own soul. When you make this a priority, you will find love, peace and joy there.

THE 10 QUESTIONS

When you try to accomplish anything, ask, "What is my highest intention?" Remember, the question is not important, but rather it is how you answer the question that matters. If you simply answer, "My highest intention is to know peace under all circumstances," then your intention will lead you to what you truly want.

Your intention is the very essence of where you will start to direct your energy. When your intention is to make the world—including your body, mind and emotions—a certain way, then your intention is to try to find happiness, fulfillment and peace through these things. On the other hand, if your intention is to know peace regardless of the external and internal world and to simply live life to its fullest, you will not only know peace, but your life will continually improve.

When you are at peace within, your life can only get better. People are afraid that if they let go and only want peace within, their life will fall apart. There is this insane

PEACE UNDER ALL CIRCUMSTANCES

belief that if we are not in control of the world that it will not continue to function properly. This is not the case at all. Ask yourself, "Do I make babies?" "Do I digest my food?" "Do I heal my wounds?"

You know how to have sex, but you have no idea how to make a baby. You know how to chew, but you would have no idea how to digest food and turn it into a body. And you know how to put on a bandage, but you have no idea how to cause cells to repair to form new skin. It is not all that hard to see that most of the universe is happening without you doing a thing. The secret to peace is to know that life will continue on when you are living in peace, and the beauty is that it will only get better when you are.

Our efforts to find happiness in the world only lead us further from our true selves. Our attempts to find love from others only make us feel more deficient within ourselves. Even when we seem to have made the world and others in it the way we want them to be, we live in constant fear that

THE 10 QUESTIONS

they will change because in our hearts we know they will.

Ask, "What is my highest intention?" and always answer "Peace—peace under all circumstances." When you do this at every moment, you will find that feeling good is not that hard to do. You already are peace. If your intention is simply to be in that place within your own Spirit, then life will continue to unfold, and you will enjoy the ride.

It is really very easy. People think they want so many things. Some people say that they do not know what they want. Those who say that they do not know are actually closer to truly knowing than those who say they know. When you do not know what you want, you most likely have come to the place where you have given up on trying to find happiness in the outside world. When you know what you want in the outside world, then you simply have not become disillusioned yet. The only thing you really want is not a thing. It is the very peace of your own soul, and it is already yours. Make knowing it your highest priority.

PEACE UNDER ALL CIRCUMSTANCES

QUESTION 10

Would I rather be right, or would I rather be happy?

"I choose to be happy."

THE 10 QUESTIONS

PEACE UNDER ALL CIRCUMSTANCES

This is the final question because if you have not felt peace from asking the other questions you are answering this one improperly. Suppose you ask Question 7, "Am I willing to let this go?" and answer, "No, I cannot let this go. It is too important to me." Well, then you are right, but are you happy?

There is no real right and wrong. There is only what is beneficial in a given context. In the context of being at peace under all circumstances, it is beneficial to choose to be happy. It is not universally wrong to choose otherwise, because no one really suffers except you because of your poor choice. In the end you have not changed anything about who you really are; you have only forgotten what you really wanted.

If you say, "No, I cannot let this go," and I tell you that you can even let *this one* go, but you believe you really cannot, then you feel you are right and I am wrong. It does not matter to me if I am wrong. I only want peace. I only want to be happy. My being right and your being wrong is

THE 10 QUESTIONS

not the source of my happiness. However, your insistence on being right is the source of your unhappiness. You suffer because you cannot let it go, and you may feel you are right, but you are not happy.

Again, it is not the question but how you answer the question. If you said, "Yes, peace is my highest priority," then why would you prefer to be right about something that does not make you happy. You only want to be right so that you can be happy anyway. Remember Question 8, "Are you coming from Spirit or from ego?" If you decided always to come from Spirit, then who is it that needs to be right? Is it you, the soul, who is insisting that you cannot let this go? You, Spirit, can always let go and have no need to be right.

You only are concerned with what is beneficial to keep experiencing more of your true nature as peace.

This last question can help in answering the other questions in ways that can lead only to peace. For example:

PEACE UNDER ALL CIRCUMSTANCES

Who am I?

If you answer that I am a human being who has a body, mind and emotions, and you are told that this is not correct and that you are pure Spirit, then who is right. If you are right that all you are is a body, mind and emotions, then you will not be at peace under all circumstances. You may be right, but you are not truly happy.

Can I handle this?

If you answer that you cannot handle any given situation, and you are told that you can handle any given situation, then who is right? If you are right that you cannot handle it, then you will not be at peace under all circumstances. You may be right, but you are not happy.

Can I be at peace with this?

If you answer that you cannot be at peace with any given situation, and you are told that you can, then who is right. If you are right that you cannot be at peace, then you will simply not be at peace. You may be right, but are you happy?

What do I feel right now?

If you do not know, then you are not experiencing life fully. If your heart is closed, then perhaps you do not know how you feel. You may be right that you do not know, but are you happy? If you are exerting effort to shield yourself from life and do not feel fully through an open heart, then you shall live in, as Gibran wrote in *The Prophet,* "...the seasonless world where you shall laugh, but not all of your laughter, and weep, but not all of your tears."

Have I suffered enough?

If you answer that you have not been suffering in your attempt to find pleasure in the world, and you are told that you are not truly at peace because of it, then who is right? You may be right that your way is working, but are you truly at peace under all circumstances? You may even insist that you have not suffered enough for your sins, and you can be right about that one if you want

PEACE UNDER ALL CIRCUMSTANCES

to be, but ask yourself, "Am I right or am I happy?"

Am I willing to let this go?

You may say that you are not and think you cannot. Then you may think you are right, but are you happy and at peace? If not, let it go.

Am I coming from Spirit or coming from ego?

You may think that your perspective is right and that another's is wrong, but ask yourself if you would rather be in the place of Spirit where you are peace or live in your ego that only is at peace when it is right. Spirit is always at peace, and ego thinks it will get peace by being right about things that seldom bring true peace.

What is my highest intention in this moment?

You may say your intention is for something other than peace, and you are told that this intention can only lead to suffering. You may insist you are right, but are you at peace?

Would I rather be right or would I rather be happy?

You can answer that I would rather be right, but then ask,

THE 10 QUESTIONS

"Am I truly happy?" If you answer "No" but you insist on choosing to be right, then that is your choice. In the end, you will have suffered enough. In your newfound humility, when you choose peace, it will be right there waiting for you.

Appendix I

Using the 10 Questions

THE 10 QUESTIONS

PEACE UNDER ALL CIRCUMSTANCES

If a specific challenge is causing you to suffer, then think of it as you go through these questions:

Who am I?

Are you this challenge before you? Remember that you are the eternal and immortal soul who is experiencing this and that you are not what you are experiencing. You are peace regardless of what is happening to your body, mind and emotions. Now just choose to come back to who you truly are when dealing with this issue. Affirm, "I am the unchanging Spirit and my true nature is pure peace."

Can I handle this?

Affirm, "Yes, I can handle this," as many times as you need to until you can feel it.

Can I be at peace with this?

Affirm, "Yes, I can be at peace with this," as many times as you need to until you can feel it.

What do I feel right now?

Check in with your felt-sense about this issue. Feel the

space below your shoulders and above your waist. Keep your heart open. Take a deep breath in, and when you exhale think, "Open." Affirm, "I am willing to go through this experience fully with an open heart, because I as Spirit can handle this and be at peace with it."

Who is experiencing this right now?

Even in the midst of the intense feelings that could come up from living with an open heart, remember that you are the observer of these feelings. Affirm, "I am the observer of these thoughts, emotions and sensations, and I am not what I experience. I am pure peace."

Have I suffered enough?

You never have to suffer, and there is no point in choosing to. Just affirm, "I have suffered enough and choose to reside in the peace of my own soul."

Am I willing to let this go?

In the end you will have to let go. If you are still suffering, it is because you are not letting go. Affirm, "As I

PEACE UNDER ALL CIRCUMSTANCES

choose peace under all circumstances, I am willing to let this go so I can dwell in the peace of my true self."

Am I coming from Spirit or ego?

If you are still suffering from this, you are still coming from ego. Affirm, "I choose to see what is happening from the vision of my soul rather than through the limited perspective of my ego."

What is my highest intention in this moment?

Remember that all you really want is peace and nothing more. Affirm, "Even though I thought I wanted this to be a certain way, in the end I only really want to be at peace right now."

Would I rather be right or would I rather be happy?

If you have come this far in this process and still are not feeling better, then ask yourself this question once again. Affirm, "I would rather be happy and am willing to let go of my need to be right. I choose peace under all circumstances because peace is who I am under all circumstances."

THE 10 QUESTIONS

Go through these questions with any problem over and over until every part of you has answered in a way that only allows for peace. The situation may not change, the past may never be again, and the future is unknown—but you can be at peace regardless.

PEACE UNDER ALL CIRCUMSTANCES

Appendix II

Meditating to Know Peace

THE 10 QUESTIONS

PEACE UNDER ALL CIRCUMSTANCES

One of the biggest secrets to establishing a state of perpetual peace is to learn to meditate in a way that establishes your own consciousness within itself. With Question 1 "Who am I?" and Question 5 "Who is experiencing this right now?" we are asked to know who we really are. However, you may still be asking, "Why is self-knowledge the key to peace under all circumstances?" The answer is really simple—You are peace!

The essence of our own being is experienced in meditation as pure peace. Our very own consciousness is peace itself. When we rest within our own true being, we know that what we are can never be taken from us. It does not matter what religious or spiritual tradition you come from and it does not matter what you believe, for if you simply bring your conscious attention back to its source, you will experience the same reality that anyone else who has engaged this experiment has also found.

Establishing consciousness back into itself is really very

THE 10 QUESTIONS

simple, and it offers us two major advantages toward living at peace in all circumstances: that we simply come to know that we are peace and that we can sit in a higher place of consciousness and observe life rather than be caught up in it. Meditation not only brings us to a state of peace, but allows us to carry that peace into every area of our life.

Other ways to say "establish consciousness within itself" are "to bring your awareness back to your very own soul" or to "know the one who is knowing" or to "be rooted in the seat of the soul, the seat of Witness Consciousness."

Although meditation is simple in this regard, it does take a bit of practice because most meditations are based on the object of consciousness and not the consciousness itself. It is easy to meditate on a candle flame, but most people find it harder and more elusive to meditate on the one who is meditating on the candle flame. Here, in the subject-object relationship, we meditate on the subject rather than the object. However, to understand who the subject is, first we

PEACE UNDER ALL CIRCUMSTANCES

can begin to discern what it is not.

The process of discerning who one truly is begins with the beautiful process of questioning that we have become so familiar with up until this point. Begin by asking:

Am I this book?

Now how do you know that you are not this book? It seems so obvious. But such questions begin to establish the simple logic that will lead us into the essence of our own being. You know you are not the book for two basic reasons:

1. If you can observe it, it cannot be you.
2. If it changes, it cannot be you.

In a subject-object relationship, the subject is not the object. The I is not the book, for the I observes the book. Even when the book changes form or is no longer there, the I is still there. If it can be observed and if it changes, it is not you. Now ask:

THE 10 QUESTIONS

Am I the surface that my body is sitting on?

The same logic applies. You are not the surface your body is sitting on because it changes and you can observe it. This is true of every single phenomenon in the material world. There is nothing in the physical world that you experience that is really the true you.

Now what about your body? Is that you? Ask:

Am I my feet?

Some people do not even have feet. If they asked that question, the obvious answer would be "No, I am not my feet as I do not even have feet and I am still here." Imagine if you removed your feet, would you still be there? You would not be able to walk as well, but you would still be there observing that your feet were gone. Your feet change constantly and you can observe them right now. If they change and you can observe them then they cannot be you. If they were removed and you were still there, then they could not be you. Now do this to your arms and legs:

PEACE UNDER ALL CIRCUMSTANCES

Am I my arms and legs?

Again the answer is no for the same reason. You are the one who observes arms and legs. They change and you can move them. If you can control something, observe something and exist when that something is absent, then that something is not you. So, now do this to your whole body:

Am I my body?

Although you may have always thought so, the same logic has to apply. You are not your body. It is a changing and temporary part of the material world, but it is not you, Spirit. This should bring an enormous amount of peace already to acknowledge that you are not a temporary and finite form that will eventually get old and sick and die.

Now ask:

Am I the sensations in the body, such as hot, cold, thirst, hunger, tension, relaxation, etc.?

Again the answer is no. You are not any sensations that you can observe and that come and go. Right now you may not feel hot and therefore you could not be hot. Or you might not feel cold, and therefore you could not be cold. Hot and cold sensations come and go, but you are still always there observing. This also helps to bring us closer to peace to know that no matter what the body feels, it is not who we really are.

Now ask:

Am I the emotions that I feel, such as anger, hurt, sadness, fear, loneliness and guilt, etc.?

Once again, the answer is no. You are not any emotion that can move through your system. You are the observer of these changing energies, and they are not you. Again, another huge step toward peace.

Now ask:

Am I my mind with its thoughts, memories, intellect and ego-sense?

As much as it seems amazing, the same logic applies, and the answer is still the same. You are not your mind. It is

PEACE UNDER ALL CIRCUMSTANCES

something you observe, but it is not you. You can hear your mind, look for your mind, stop your mind, start your mind and hear the space between your thoughts when your mind is not there.

Try it. Repeat the alphabet in your head, A, B, C, D and so on. Listen to the letters. Now stop the alphabet and listen to the silence. You are still there are you not? If you can start it, stop it, listen to it and are there when it is not, then it could not possibly be you.

So who are you then? You are what is left when the mind is quiet and no longer is telling you what you are not. You are the pure being who exists through all the changes of the body, sensations, emotions and mind. It is really important for you to find this for yourself and not just be told. To intellectually get it is not enough, because you must transcend your mind rather than simply believe what I say.

You can close your eyes at any time and go through this process. Ask if I am the sounds I hear, the chair I am sitting on, the clothing I wear, the body I feel, the sensations in the body, the emotions I feel and the mind I hear. Do this through direct experience rather than just through your intellect. Remember this is about being peace, not just believing that you are peace.

Assuming you agree with me that you are not these things, then it would be helpful to now begin understanding what you truly are through direct experience. In between these sentences that you are reading now, take a few moments to practice what you are reading.

Close your eyes and bring your attention to the blue/black space in your forehead. Notice how you can be aware of this space above and between your two physical eyes. Try to identify the "I Am" presence that is gazing into this space.

You are aware that you are aware. This is what we call the "seat of the soul." It is where the consciousness comes to experience itself as consciousness itself.

A human being has four major levels:

PEACE UNDER ALL CIRCUMSTANCES

1. The Body and its Sensations
2. The Emotions
3. The Mind
4. The Soul

What you are now learning to do is to bring your attention to the soul rather than the body, mind or emotions. Become aware of the one who hears these words as you read or listen to them being read. Who is it that hears?

This is the object of our meditation and the true source of peace. You are learning to meditate on the unchanging Spirit that you are rather than on the changing forms and energies that you experience. You are becoming rooted in the "I Am," which is the subject of a subject-object relationship.

Now close your eyes again and take a deep breath while focusing on the space in your forehead. As you exhale, just relax your body. Notice how you instantly come back into the present moment where you truly exist. The soul is not in the past or the future—it exists as your true self right here

THE 10 QUESTIONS

now. All you have to do is bring your attention there instead of keeping it on the external things that it observes.

We now make a clear distinction between outside and inside. Outside includes anything that moves, changes or vibrates, including body, mind and emotions. Inside is simply in the peace of your own being as the soul.

Meditation is very simple, and here are the few basics you need to get started:

1. Commit to practicing every day—morning and evening—for at least five minutes.
2. Sit in a comfortable position with your spine erect, and sit so that you can remain awake and alert.
3. Bring your attention to the space in your forehead, and keep coming back to it when you get caught in your thinking.
4. Do not try to stop your thoughts or your emotions. Just keep coming back to the "I Am" presence. Meditation is not about stopping your thoughts. Meditation is

PEACE UNDER ALL CIRCUMSTANCES

about transcending your thoughts.

5. When you inhale, repeat in your mind, "I Am."
6. When you exhale, repeat in your mind, "Peace."
7. Inhale and think "I Am." Exhale and think "Peace." While you are sitting and your mind wanders, come back to the inner space and to the words coordinated with the breathing.

This practice is obviously very basic, and the levels will go deeper. However, for now, this is the essence of any good meditation practice where consciousness is becoming established in itself. You simply bring your attention to the soul itself and repeat something in your mind that helps you to become established there. You are not trying to stop your mind; you are simply engaging the practice. When you get caught up in your mind and your mind wanders, then just gently and compassionately come back to the practice.

It is very important to practice this every day so that

THE 10 QUESTIONS

you can become established in the soul instead of just believing in it. When you do this, you will be able to observe what is happening in the world without getting caught up in it. If you combine a regular meditation practice with the regular use of The 10 Questions, then peace will be the inevitable result.

Appendix III

Surrendering to Life

THE 10 QUESTIONS

It is impossible to be at peace under all circumstances if we resist Life. Life is what is happening to us at every moment. It has been happening to us since birth, and it will happen to us until death. It began happening to us the moment we came into the body, and it will continue to happen to us until the time we leave the body. We are guests here, and no visitor stays forever.

The secret to being at peace with everything that happens here on Earth is simply to see it in its proper perspective and then to enjoy the show. Life has been happening long before you got here, and it will happen for many more years after you leave. You are here for a very short period of time and there is really no reason to get distressed over it.

While you are here, people will be born and people will die. Bodies will be born, grow, get sick, get old and die. Freedom and peace do not require changing this, they require being okay with this. In fact, they require the choice to be exceptionally excited about all this.

PEACE UNDER ALL CIRCUMSTANCES

Life is an incredible 3-D movie full of every story you could possibly imagine. You have a front row seat. Are you enjoying it? You can. If you've answered The 10 Questions properly and you are established in the seat of your higher consciousness, then you really can. Remember you are peace and are eternally free. You are pure consciousness and pure joy. You are entitled to remain rooted in your true nature while life unfolds. All you have to do is go along for the ride.

It is like finding yourself being born in a boat on a river. You have no idea how you got there, and you have no idea where the river is going. You are like an amnesia victim who just ended up somewhere and has no idea where he came from. You could begin flipping out and trying to paddle back upstream or you could try to paddle faster to try to get to the end sooner. You could try to anchor or grab rocks and trees. You could become afraid of where the river is going or what obstacle you might encounter next. You could ruin the

THE 10 QUESTIONS

entire journey and spend it in fear and misery.

Or you could just stop and breathe and enjoy yourself right where you are. You could let go of the past (trying to paddle back upstream to where you liked it better) or try to paddle faster (to get to a potentially more desirable future), or you could just lift up your paddle and be honored to be having this experience. Think of how nice it would be to know you are not the river, the boat or the paddle, but are the one who could just sit back, relax and be at peace with the journey.

Surrendering to life is just like pulling your oar out of the water and seeing where you end up. You might say that you are not willing to take the chance because you might not get what you want or you might get hurt. Remember that you are the soul, not the body, mind or emotions. When something in your head says, "But I might get hurt or not get what I want," ask yourself, "Who is it that is saying these things?" Is it your mind or your soul? If you can hear

PEACE UNDER ALL CIRCUMSTANCES

it, can it be you?

When you are fulfilled from within, you are just excited to see what happens next in life. You have come to realize that nothing outside is going to make you happy, peaceful and free anyway. You have suffered enough with that game and now just want to enjoy the rest of your time on the river.

There is something amazing about the river when you let go and surrender to it. It somehow knows where it is going, and it is taking you along with it. To let go does not mean to get left behind. It does not mean you will end up broke, sick and alone. It might, but you are okay with that now. It means that all rivers eventually lead to the ocean, and you are trusting in the flow. Trust does not mean that you will get what you want. Trust means that you would much rather let life lead than your own ego.

You can listen to your emotionally disturbed heart and your chaotic mind to try to run your life, or you can become established in the soul and allow Life to run your life. This just means that you do what needs to be done. It means that you act appropriately in every moment, engaging what the moment asks of you. If you are a mother, be a mother. If you are a doctor, be a doctor. Surrender does not mean to drop everything and do nothing. It means that you see clearly what is and respond appropriately to it.

In this you have to be willing to let go of what your ego mind tells you that it wants, or what it thinks will make you happy. You learn to observe that thing, rather than thinking that you are that thing. You let go of its likes, preferences, wants, hopes, dreams and goals. At first this is scary, but in the end, just ask, "Am I coming from Spirit or ego?" All personal preferences are of the ego, and honestly you do not want them.

Ask yourself, "Does my preference for whether I die or not really matter?" Does not wanting this really change anything? Does your preference for not paying taxes actually keep you from having to pay them? Death and taxes! These

PEACE UNDER ALL CIRCUMSTANCES

are not the only things you can choose to surrender to. Why not surrender to all of it? How does resisting it make it any better? Resisting it only makes you afraid and miserable. When it is appropriate to change something, you do it—not because you prefer to, but because it is what the moment is asking for.

People are terrified of letting go because of a deep sense of personal responsibility. They fail to understand that when they cease to function from the worrying mind that they can begin functioning from the immortal soul. The soul is pure wisdom, pure power and pure love. There is nothing that it cannot handle, and there is nothing that it cannot enjoy. The soul already knows what is appropriate and already holds the very clear knowledge of how your life is unfolding.

People believe that in letting go of the goals, preferences and dreams of the ego that they will not get anywhere. This is entirely backward. The soul has vision, not goals. The soul clearly can see a long-term, mid-range and short-term vision, but it does not believe that it needs to manifest these things to be happy. It just knows it is here on Earth with something to do while it is here. It knows what this mission is. Which is to say that you do know what your purpose in life is. If you think you do not, you just have too many extra thoughts in which you have been caught up. When you reestablish yourself in the soul, you will know exactly what to do in every moment, and you will have a life vision that will seem wonderfully fulfilling.

My experience is that letting go is always the answer. I have never let go of my ego-mind and found myself worse off. The more I let go of this lower self, the more the Divine Self can manifest. It was scary at first, but now it is always wonderful to just keep releasing and becoming more and more free. Remember freedom is not to get what your mind wants, but to be free of the mind that wants. When you realize that you can want and need nothing, then you truly get to enjoy your life and know what being fulfilled really

PEACE UNDER ALL CIRCUMSTANCES

means.

In this state, nothing needs to be added, and nothing needs to be taken away. You simply let go and rest in what is. Joyfully you find that in that moment everything you ever wanted to feel is right there as it always was.

THE 10 QUESTIONS

Appendix IV

Opening the Heart and Working Effectively with Emotions

THE 10 QUESTIONS

PEACE UNDER ALL CIRCUMSTANCES

It is easy to say that a person can be at peace when the emotional heart and mind are in turmoil; however, it is far harder to do in reality. It is also easy to say, "Keep your heart open under all circumstances," and so too this is easier said than done. The path to freedom is not always easy, but in the end the same basic principles apply whether we like it or not.

A few prerequisites for profound spiritual growth are:

1. Know who you are as Spirit and live from that space.
2. Surrender to life and just go along for the ride.
3. Keep your heart open and experience the journey to its fullest.

We have discussed the need to remain centered in the space of peace for peace to be there all of the time. We have talked about surrendering to life so that you can just enjoy it rather than fight it. However, what we still need to look into further is what to do with our minds and emotions when we

THE 10 QUESTIONS

are working to become truly free.

When we surrender to life and learn to observe from the seat of Witness Consciousness, we instantly find that our lower self begins to throw a fit. When we stop living from our personal preferences and do what life is asking from us, our emotions have a funny way of rising up to the surface. It is as if we told a child that he can no longer have his way every second of the day. Now just imagine how upset he would be.

Our hearts are like this. When we tell our heart that we will observe it but not act out on it, our heart can begin to get very loud. Remember that we are told to observe our emotions and to realize that these are not who we really are. If we have come to see that we are not that scared person inside, then why would we base our life on it? The truth is that we do not want to base our life around that scared, angry, hurt and lonely part. All it will do is create more and more of its old patterns. Therefore, in becoming free, we really do need

PEACE UNDER ALL CIRCUMSTANCES

to understand our relationship to our inner being.

The heart as referred to here is associated with our emotions and the sensations that go with these emotions. We feel these things usually below our shoulders and above our waist. We all know what these energies are like because we live with them every day. These energies cause our minds to talk incessantly about how to feel better and seem to infiltrate all our relationships and interactions. These energies are the cause of so much grief and unfortunately most of us do not know how to deal with them.

The first thing to understand about the heart and its feelings is that we are meant to feel what is in there. It is part of life to have emotions. Freedom is not the ability to be without fear; it is the ability to be okay when fear is passing through the system. The system is an organism—an animal—with many mechanisms in place to ensure its survival. You are not this animal, but you are certainly experiencing this world through it.

THE 10 QUESTIONS

The human animal has all kinds of fear, anger, hurt, sadness, guilt, jealousy, insecurity and even hatred and rage. It is important to acknowledge that these feelings are there, but we do not have to call them "ours." You do not really have to say that that is your fear, anger and sadness. There is just fear, anger and sadness in the system. Can you handle this?

It's there, but when you say, "No, I cannot handle it," you do one of two things. You either try to suppress it and push it away or deny it, or you act out on it in an attempt to try to feel better. These two mechanisms of suppression and expression do not work. Pushing the emotions away blocks up the system and causes the emotions to stay there forever. To act out on the emotions only reinforces them and makes them worse.

Let's say you are angry with someone, and you deny your feelings and suppress them. Now next week when that person does the same thing again, you are angrier than you were the first time. Bottling up your anger and closing your heart just

PEACE UNDER ALL CIRCUMSTANCES

that much more only hurts you in the long run, because you will never be free of your anger that way.

Suppose you decide to express your emotions because you conclude that it is not beneficial to suppress them. Now you begin to let out your feelings and tell those around you how you feel and how they should be. Will you be more or less angry when they do the same things again? The truth is that you will be angrier at someone if you express your emotions toward them and they repeat the same patterns.

Suppressing your emotions strengthens them and acting out only makes them worse. The real secret of what to do is simply to do nothing. When emotions come up, just keep your heart open and feel the emotions. These are just energies passing before your consciousness. You do not have to do anything about them. Effectively working with emotions means that you do not work with them at all. Simply sit in the seat of your own soul and watch as they come up.

As you do, you will feel things like you have never felt

them before. You will truly get to know what you have been holding down in your heart for so many years. Now the stuff is coming up, and it will go away if you know what to do with it. Emotions are temporary and fleeting energies that pass before your consciousness. Emotions are not eternal and will not remain if you let them pass. The emotions that are stored within your system can be removed so they do not keep coming up over and over again as the same patterns. This does not mean that you will never have emotions. It only means that the old ones that were meant to pass will have passed, and you will not live every day with things that could have long since been gone.

The answer to the question of how to be at peace under all circumstances even when the heart and mind are in great pain is to feel it fully when it is coming up. You simply pull back into the seat of Witness Consciousness and remember to do three things:

1. Relax your body.

PEACE UNDER ALL CIRCUMSTANCES

2. Keep breathing.

3. Just feel what is coming up.

When you do this, you are making space for what needs to come through. You cannot avoid these feelings, but you can allow them to be there so they can pass when it is their time to pass. Every time you do this, the feelings will be less and less intense. There is a temporary and limited amount of stuff that was stored in the heart from your past. All you have to do is relax your body, keep your breathing moving, and feel the feelings as they come up while sitting in the seat of higher consciousness. The emotions will burn themselves away, and your heart will become clearer and clearer each day.

In time new waves of love, light and peace will flow through your system for no reason at all. Old emotional knots that clogged the system will be gone, and energy flows like you have never known before will begin to awaken. You will literally experience states of being previously beyond your comprehension. Because certain channels within you were

THE 10 QUESTIONS

always blocked, you never had the full, delicious experiences of which you are capable.

The human experience really can be ecstatic. The experience of your soul is always ecstatic as it transcends time and space, so that no matter what is happening in life, you are free and at peace. In time even the human system comes back to balance, and you find an amazing peace right there within your heart. When the heart is kept unconditionally open, it clears itself out. This is not easy or necessarily fun, especially in the beginning, but in time it does get easier and the periods of feeling amazing become more and more pronounced.

An open and clear heart is full of the same love, peace and bliss as Spirit. At first we need to transcend the human system so that we can get out of the way of its emotional and mental purification process. In time when the cleansing is done, we get to rest in our hearts in total peace. Nothing can bring back the old emotional blockages. The old buttons

PEACE UNDER ALL CIRCUMSTANCES

that people could push are gone. In this state it is possible for fear, anger or sadness to arise, but the emotions pass through very quickly and leave no trace. We become open channels, and life just passes right through us.

In this state of profound freedom, we just live life. There is no attainment and no goal. We are complete and just live in peace. Life keeps happening, and we are truly enjoying the ride. The body remains free of any psychosomatic illness, the heart remains generally happy, the mind is clear and focused, and the soul rests comfortably within itself in absolute peace. This state is real, and it is available for anyone who does the work required to be free.

It is not always easy to reverse years of old patterns, but there is no other work to do. The question is, "Are you at peace at every moment or not?" If you are not, then you simply set the intention, "I am going to be at peace at every moment and under all circumstances." Once you've said it, now reclaim it—for it is yours to claim.

THE 10 QUESTIONS

ABOUT THE AUTHOR

Matthew Brownstein, CIHt is the CEO of Anahat Education Group, Inc., President of the International Association of Interpersonal Hypnotherapists (IAIH), and the Founder and Executive Director of the Institute of Interpersonal Hypnotherapy (formerly the Florida Institute of Hypnotherapy), Florida's first State-Licensed Postsecondary Vocational Hypnotherapy Institute through the Florida Department of Education. Matthew is also the founder of Silent Light Publishers.

Matthew began as a Certified Clinical Hypnotherapist in 1997 and since then has logged over 18,000 hours of clinical and classroom experience. In 2007, Matthew opened as the Florida Institute of Hypnotherapy, which has since expanded and grown into multiple States across the nation with graduates now spanning the entire globe.

PEACE UNDER ALL CIRCUMSTANCES

Matthew is the author of *Interpersonal Hypnotherapy, Peace Under All Circumstances, The Sacred Geometry of Meditation, The Sutras on Healing and Enlightenment* and *The Anahat Meditation System*. He has also published over 60 audio products in the fields of Hypnotherapy, Personal Growth and Spiritual Development.

Made in the USA
San Bernardino, CA
19 April 2017